12 AWESOME WOMEN EXPLORERS YOU'VE NEVER HEARD OF

Lynn Schreiber

Find out about other awesome women you've never heard of on

www.jumpmag.co.uk

For Thomas

INTRODUCTION

The teacher clapped her hands, and waited for the chatter to fade.

"Children, for this week's homework, I'd like you to research a famous explorer and write a short essay about their adventure", she announced.

Lucy packed away her school supplies and fastened her bag. On her way home, she and her friends discussed their homework assignment.

"Who are you going to write about?", asked Lucy.

Her friend Sarah frowned, "I'm not sure. An explorer – she means someone like Captain Cook or Columbus, right?"

"Well, I guess it could be a modern explorer, like an astronaut or someone who sailed around the world. Ms Williams didn't say", replied Lucy. "I'll google for some ideas when I get home".

Later that evening Lucy stared in confusion at the computer screen. Something was very odd. She'd checked several websites, using various combinations of 'world explorers' and 'famous explorers', and she could only find men.

"Mum. Can you come and look? Why are there no women explorers in these lists?", she asked.

"You have to remember, many of these explorers came from a time when women weren't allowed to vote, or even to travel freely. Women couldn't just go and discover the world, and those who did weren't talked or written about as much as the men. Try googling 'women explorers' and see what you find then', Lucy mother suggested.

"Oh, this site looks interesting. Here's an female astronaut, and this woman explored Egypt, and was an architect and a spy! Why don't the history books report on that? Look, the first woman to climb Mount Everest!', Lucy exclaimed, as she started to scribble some notes.

An hour later, Lucy was engrossed in a thrilling tale of adventure in South America when her mother popped her head around the door, "It's almost time for bed, Lucy. How did you get on with your homework?".

"Almost done, Mum. I found so many great stories, it

was hard to decide which woman to put in my report!",
Lucy replied. "The story of Gudrid, the medieval
explorer from Iceland, is my favourite. She was one of
the first Europeans to travel to North America, long
before Columbus!".

GUDRID THORBJARNARDOTTIR

JUMP! MAG

Gudrid Thorbjarnardottir gave birth to the first European to be born in North America

Gudrid Thorbjarnardottir
Viking Explorer
Sailed to North America almost 500 years before Columbus

If you think that Gudrid's name is difficult to pronounce in English, then try it in the language of the country where she lived - *Guðríður Þorbjarnardóttir*. Some letters of the Icelandic alphabet don't exist in English,

5

so we will have to call her Gudrid!

Gudrid is often said to have been the most travelled woman of the Middle Ages, travelling from her homeland of Iceland to Greenland and then on to North America, almost 500 years before Christopher Columbus.

Born the granddaughter of a slave, and the daughter of farmers in the pagan, pre-Christian era, Gudrid travelled with her father to Greenland, to accompany Erik the Red, who founded the first Norse settlement there. Gudrid married Thorstein, one of Erik the Red's sons.

Following the lead of Thorstein's brother Leif Eriksson, Gudrid and her husband sailed to North America. Leif Eriksson is believed to have been the first European to have visited North America. On the return journey to Greenland, Thorstein died and Gudrid stayed there, marrying a second time.

Gudrid returned to Vinland, as they called North America, with her second husband, the merchant Thorfinnr Karlsefni in the year 1010. They led an expedition of three ships and 160 settlers.

They remained in North America for several years, and

during this time Gudrid gave birth to a son, Snorri Thorfinnsson, who is thought to be the first European born in the Americas. Eventually, the Norse invaders were repelled by the Native Americans, and Gudrid and her family returned to Greenland, taking with them vines, grapes, pelts and other valuable items.

Karlsefni, Gudrid and Snorri returned to Iceland, where the family's second son, Thorbjorn was born. It was many years before Gudrid would go exploring again - not until her husband Karlsefni had died, and her sons had married.

Around this time, Iceland and Greenland became Christian, and so Gudrid decided to go on a pilgrimage to Rome. She visited the Vatican, and is thought to have even met the Pope, before returning again to Greenland, where her son built her a church. She became a nun and anchoress and lived there until her death.

Much of what what we know about Gudrid comes from the Vinland Sagas - written about 200 to 300 years after Gudrid's time; the Saga of the Greenlanders (*Grænlendinga Saga*) and The Saga of Eric the Red, (*Eiríks Saga Rauða*).

For many years, historians argued whether the sagas

were fictional, but the discovery of two important archaeological sites seems to suggest that the sagas were based on real events. Viking houses found in L'Anse aux Meadows, Canada and in Glaumbaer, Iceland were of similar size and build. In both places, archaeologists discovered items that would have been used by women, such as spindles and knitting needles.

The Vinland Sagas describe Gudrid as being an intelligent woman of striking appearance, who knew how to conduct herself among strangers. She was certainly one of the most widely travelled women of her time, and an inspiration to later explorers.

LADY EVELYN COBBOLD

JUMP! MAG

"When I look into my journal I shall live it all again. Time cannot rob me of the memories that I treasure in my heart... the countless pilgrims who passed me with shining eyes of faith, the wonder and glory of the Haram of Makkah, the great pilgrimage through the desert and the hills to Arafaat, and above all the abiding sense of joy and fulfilment that possesses the soul."

Lady Evelyn Cobbold
Writer

First British Woman to Make Pilgrimage to Mecca

Lady Evelyn Cobbold was born in Edinburgh on 17 July 1867. Her father was the 7th Earl of Dunmore, and her mother Lady Gertrude Coke, daughter of the 2nd Earl of Leicester. Lady Evelyn's father loved to travel, and the family spent the winter months in a villa on a hill outside Algiers. She learned Arabic from the local servants, and her favourite past-time was to escape her governess and visit local mosques with her Algerian friends. She later said that she was always 'a little Muslim at heart'.

In 1891, Lady Evelyn married John Dupuis Cobbold, in the city of Cairo, Egypt, returning to John's home in Suffolk, England, where they brought up their three children. It wasn't long before Lady Evelyn returned to her travels, and in 1912 she published a memoir of her adventures, titled 'Wayfarers in the Libyan Dessert'.

Lady Evelyn could not remember converting to Islam, later writing,

"I am often asked when and why I became a Muslim. I can only reply that I do not know the precise moment when the truth of Islam dawned upon me. It seems that I have always been a Muslim".

She wrote of visiting Rome with friends, and going to meet the Pope. When she was asked by the Pope if she were Catholic, she replied that she was a Muslim. She noted that she surprised herself by this announcement, as she had not thought about Islam for many years, but 'a match was lit and I then and there determined to read up and study the Faith'.

After Lady Evelyn and her husband separated, she was given the Glencarron Estate in Scotland, where she lived for many years, enjoying the wide open spaces, and the hunt. After the death of her husband in 1929, she started to plan for the Hajj.

The Hajj is a ritual journey to Saudi Arabia to worship in the holy city of Mecca. It is one of the five pillars of Islam, central to the faith, and which every Muslim is expected to undertake at least once in their lifetime, if they can afford it, and are physically able to do so.

In 1933, when Lady Evelyn finally was able to journey to Mecca, she joined tens of thousands of pilgrims. Nowadays, that number had swelled to more than 2 million! It is now the largest yearly gathering of people in the world, bringing together Muslims of all nationalities and skin colours.

Lady Evelyn, or to use her Muslim name, Sayyidah Zainab, was overwhelmed by the sight of fellow worshippers from all over the world. After her return to Scotland, she published a book about her journey; Pilgrimage to Mecca.

"Two hundred and fifty miles [400 km] from Jeddah to Medina took us fifteen hours to accomplish and I take off my hat to the little Ford that gallantly carried us through those sandy wastes.... Besides the pilgrims on camels, we met many on foot, toiling slowly through the scorching desert with water jugs in their hands clad in their Ihram (or two towels), and, as they were bare headed, many carried umbrellas. Ten days is the usual time it takes a camel to accomplish the journey between Medina and Jeddah and three weeks for the pilgrim on foot...."

The year after her journey to Mecca, she travelled through Europe with her grandson, Toby Sladen, crossed the Mediterranean and flew down the Nile to Kenya. The trip was published in a book called 'Kenya, the Land of Illusions'.

Lady Evelyn's final years were spent in her Scottish estate, Glencarron, where she died in 1963, at the age of 95. Her final wish, "to be buried where the stags will run over my grave", was granted. Bringing together her Scottish roots, and her faith, she'd instructed that a piper play, and requested that Sheikh Muhammad Tufail, the imam of the Woking Mosque in London read a specific verse from the Surah Al Nur (Light). "Allah is the Light of the heavens and the earth,".

As the first British-born woman to perform the Hajj pilgrimage to Mecca, Lady Evelyn stepped well outside her traditional roots, and explored a culture far from her homeland.

MAE JEMISON

JUMP! MAG

I am as much a part
of this universe as
any speck of stardust

Mae Jemison
Astronaut
First African-American woman in space

Born on 17 October 1956 in Alabama, but brought up in Chicago, USA, Mae Jemison said later that she just *knew* as a child that she would go into space. During her school years, Mae was torn between pursuing an academic career, or becoming a dancer. Her mother told her, "You can always dance if you're a doctor, but you can't doctor if you're a dancer", and so Mae's destiny was set!

"When I went to school for engineering and medicine, it wasn't because I wanted to be the new role model. I wanted to help determine the future of engineering, medicine and outer space"

Mae worked as a doctor after her training, both in USA and in Africa - travelling to Sierra Leone to work with the Peace Corps organisation. In 1987 she was selected by NASA to join the astronaut corps, and went into orbit aboard the Space Shuttle Endeavour on 12 September 1992. She recalls looking out of the window of Endeavour, and the first thing she saw was her beloved hometown, Chicago.

Travelling with Mae on the Space Shuttle were representatives of those who she says are often left out. She took a poster of the dance production 'Cry' by the Alvin Ailey American Dance Company, a Bundu statue from the African country of Sierra Leone, and a certificate from the Chicago Public School for the school children who work to improve their science and maths.

She took these objects to signal that space belongs to everyone, and because they represent human creativity. The creativity that was required to "conceive and build and launch the space shuttle, springs from the same source as the imagination and analysis it took to carve a Bundu statue, or the ingenuity it took to design, choreograph, and stage Cry", she said afterwards.

After leaving NASA, Mae continued to work in the field of science, and to dance. An avid fan of the series, which she credits as inspiring her to become a space traveller, Mae appeared in an episode of Star Trek, and met her idol Nichelle Nichols, who played Uhura.

You may have heard people say that a person is a "geek" or an "artist", but Mae firmly believes that you can both at the same time - and she is living proof!

In 2012, Mae started the 100YSS programme, which aims to foster scientific research, and to connect technology to our everyday life. Space isn't just for rocket science and billionaires, she insists, we are all involved in the science of space - just look at the GPRS map technology on your smartphone!

Mae Jemison was the first African American woman in space, but to reduce her life's work to this one statistic would be a great mistake. She is a seriously impressive role model for girls around the world.

GERTRUDE BELL

"Have I ever told you what the river is like on a hot summer night?

At dusk the mist hangs in long white bands over the water; the twilight fades and the lights of the town shine out on either bank, with the river, dark and smooth and full of mysterious reflections, like a road of triumph through the midst"

Gertrude Bell
Writer, Archaeologist, Spy
Co-Author of Iraq Constitution, Founder of Iraqi Museum

In a time when women were discouraged from travelling, and forbidden from voting, Gertrude Bell was a pioneer. She was born into a wealthy family in County Durham, England, and attended school in London before going on to win a first class degree at

Oxford University – the first woman in modern times to achieve this honour.

After leaving Oxford, Gertrude travelled extensively. She developed a love for mountaineering in the Swiss Alps, and even had an Alpine peak named after her – the Gertrudespitze. She embarked on not one but two around-the-world trips; one in 1897 -1898 and another in 1902 -1903.

In the late 1800s, Gertrude travelled through the Ottoman Empire. Gertrude had a deep affection for the Arab peoples, learning their languages, exploring their archaeological sites and travelling for thousands of miles through the deserts. She was one of the first Western women to visit many areas, and was respected by the leaders of the tribes she met. Unlike male travellers, Gertrude was allowed access to the women of the tribes, which gave her a more rounded understanding of their culture.

In 1905 she published a book called *The Desert and the Sown*, about her travels through Syria to Asia Minor, and in 1907 her study on the Byzantine church ruins in Binbirkilise was published in the book *A Thousand and One Churches*.

The Ottoman Empire joined Germany, Austria-Hungary and Bulgaria as the Central Powers in their fight against the Allies in World War I. Gertrude's knowledge of the Arab countries and their tribes was of interest to the British Intelligence services; she was recruited to be a spy, and asked to create maps of the area. She worked out the route that enabled the British army to reach Baghdad safely.

After the war, the Ottoman Empire finally collapsed, and the remaining states were divided into a several new states. Gertrude wrote an important policy document, detailing the political and societal systems in Mesopotamia, an area which included modern-day Iraq, Kuwait, and parts of Syria, Turkey and Iran. She worked closely with T.E. Lawrence (better known as Lawrence of Arabia), and the Oriental Secretary Percy Cox.

At the Cairo Conference in 1920, Gertrude and Lawrence highly recommended Faisal bin Hussein as the new King of Iraq. When Faisal arrived in Baghdad, Gertrude advised him on local issues, including matters involving tribal geography and local business, and even designed the new Iraqi flag. It would not be until 1932 that the Kingdom of Iraq was granted independence from UK.

Gertrude turned her attention to her first great love – archaeology. In 1922, she began gathering important artefacts in a government building in Baghdad, in order to prevent them being taken from the country. In 1926, the Iraqi government moved the collection to a new building, and named Gertrude as museum's director of the Baghdad Archaeological Museum. The museum still exists, now named the National Museum of Iraq.

Gertrude Bell died in Baghdad in 1926, shortly before her 58th birthday. Gertrude was a powerful force in the politics of the Middle East, and is often referred to as the 'kingmaker' of Iraq. Her extraordinary accomplishments live on in her wonderful letters and diaries, which can be read online at the Gertrude Bell Archive of Newcastle University.

JUMP! MAG

"Call me the free spirit of the mountains"

Junko Tabei
Mountaineer
First Woman to Summit Mount Everest

Junko Tabei was born on 23 May 1939 in the Fukishimo province of North Japan, one of six children in her family. She was often unwell as a child, as she suffered from weak lungs. She wasn't very athletic, and disliked sports.

When Junko was 10 years old, she joined a school climbing trip to Mount Asahi and Mount Chausu. She loved that climbing wasn't a competitive sport, and that she could climb at her own pace.

After graduating from Showa Women's University, Junko joined mountain climbing clubs, and in 1969 she established the Ladies Climbing Club: Japan. Even though women in Japan had been allowed to vote since 1946, it was still considered unacceptable for them to go out to work - that was only for men!

When Junko and fifteen fellow climbers began organising the Japanese Women's Everest Expedition, they were told they should stay home and raise children. Despite this opposition, the group set off to Nepal in early 1975. The Japanese climbers were accompanied by nine local Sherpa people, including the experienced guide Ang Tshering, who was to climb with Junko. On May 16 1975 Junko and Ang reached the summit of Mount Everest.

She has continued to climb, becoming the first woman in the world to reach the highest mountain on each of the seven continents.

1975 - Mt. Everest, on the border of Tibet and Nepal, Asia.

1981 - Mt. Kilimanjaro - Tanzania, Africa.

1987 - Mt. Aconcagua, Argentina, South America.

1988 - Mt. Denali, USA, North America.

1991 - Mt. Vinson, Antartica.

1992 - Mt. Carstensz Pyramid, Indonesia.

1992 - Mt. Elbrus, Russia, Europe.

When Junko climbed Everest in 1975, the Nepalese government restricted access to the mountain, only allowing a certain amount of climbers a year. Since then, these restrictions have been lifted, and more and more people have streamed to the area to attempt the climb. Alarmed by the damage inflicted on the area, Junko has been campaigning for many years to protect and preserve mountain regions.

In 1990, she founded the Himalayan Adventure Trust - Japan, which has been active in a number of fields, including the collection of rubbish, and the building of incinerators, planting apple trees to make cash income for Himalayan villagers, and the organisation of international youth exchanges for the conservation of mountain environments.

Junko has been called a 'housewife climber' and an 'Everest mommy', but in her own words…

"Call me the free spirit of the mountains".

LOUISE BOYD

"I had the feeling of regret that isolation combined with danger made this beauty inaccessible and known to so few"

Louise Boyd
Polar Explorer
First Woman on Board of National Geographic Society

Louise Boyd was born in California, USA, on 16 September 1887. After her parents died in 1920, when she was 32 years old, Louise inherited a fortune, and resolved to use it to explore the world.

years until the outbreak of World War II, exploring and mapping the coast of Greenland. Due to the war, she was forced to delay the publication of her latest book. She was asked by the US government to lead an expedition along the west coast of Greenland.

The one regret that Louise had, was that she had not travelled to the North Pole. In 1955, she hired an airplane and achieved her childhood dream.

"North, north, north we flew. Soon we left all land behind us. From the cabin window I saw great stretches of ocean flecked with patches of white floating ice. Now the ice became denser, its jagged edges surrounding open pools of sea. And as I saw the ocean change to massive fields of solid white, my heart leaped up. I knew we were approaching my goal.

Then -- in a moment of happiness which I shall never forget -- our instruments told me we were there. For directly below us, 9,000 feet down, lay the North Pole!"

In 1960, Louise was the first woman to be elected to the board of the US Geographical Society. Louise died in 1972, two days before her 85th birthday.

She is often said to be 'the first woman to fly over the

North Pole', but her true legacy remains her incredible scientific expeditions and research in one of the world's most challenging environments.

BESSIE COLEMAN

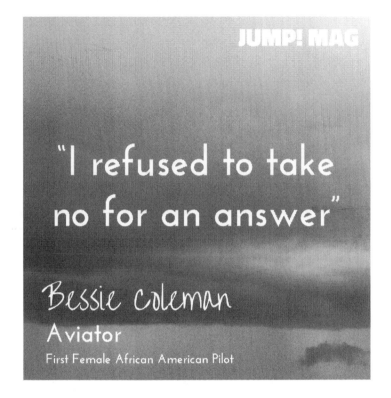

"I refused to take no for an answer"

Bessie Coleman
Aviator
First Female African American Pilot

JUMP! MAG

Bessie Coleman grew up in the segregated south of USA. At the time of her birth in 1892, African American children and adults were not allowed to use the same schools as whites, or ride on the same buses. Many children didn't even go to school. Bessie went to an all black school from the age of six years, and was particularly good at maths. During the cotton harvest, Bessie and her friends had to work in the fields, instead of going to school.

Once she had completed school, Bessie wanted to go on to learn more. She used her savings to attend University in Oklahoma, but after a year she ran out of money, and was forced to return home to Texas.

In 1915, Bessie decided to move north to Chicago, where discrimination was less severe. She worked as a manicurist in a beauty shop for several years, but she never gave up on her aim to "amount to something". She was intrigued by soldiers returning from World War I, who told wild tales of aviators. Her brother would tease her by saying that French women were superior to African American women, because they could fly, so Bessie decided to prove him wrong!

She approached a number of flying schools in USA, but none of them accepted her - at that time there were very few women pilots, and Bessie's African American heritage made it even more difficult for her to find acceptance.

Determined not to give up, Bessie searched for ways to

follow her dream. Robert Abbott, owner of a Chicago newspaper, and one of the first African American millionaires, advised Bessie to go to a French flying school. After learning to speak French, and with the support of Abbot and other African American entrepreneurs, Bessie set off for Paris in November 1920.

For seven months, Bessie worked hard, learning tail spins, banking and loop the loop, before receiving her pilots licence from the Federation Aeronautique Internationale in 1921. She spent another three months training before heading back to USA in September of that year.

She was surprised by the public interest in her achievement, but soon realised that if she wished to earn her living as an aviator, she would need additional skills. There wasn't nearly as much call for pilots back then, as airplane travel was still very unusual, and as an African American woman, not much chance of her getting hired! That only left her the option of 'barnstorming', displaying her flying skills in an airshow. She spent another six months in France, honing her skills before returning to New York in August 1922.

Bessie's first appearance was in an airshow at Curtiss Field, near New York, where she was presented to the public as "the world's greatest woman flyer". For several years, Bessie appeared in airshows around the country, delighting the crowd with her daring feats. Bessie's dream was to open a flying school, and she presented a series of lectures to encourage other African Americans to learn to fly. She refused to appear at events that were segregated, forcing the organisers to allow all visitors to enter through the same gates.

With the help of her supporters, Bessie was able to buy a plane, which she had transported to Jacksonville for an event. On the evening of April 30 1926, Bessie and her mechanic took the plane up in a test flight. It was to be their last. A mechanical malfunction caused the plane to flip, and both Bessie and the mechanic died. Thousands of people attended Bessie's memorial service and funeral.

In 1929, her dream of establishing a flying school became a reality, when William J Powell established the Bessie Coleman Aero Club in Los Angeles. Now other African American women and men could follow in Bessie's footsteps, and learn to fly.

VICTORIA DRUMMOND

"As we sailed south, the nights became hot and the sky dark and velvety, sprinkled with a myriad of stars... little droves of silvery flying fish skimmed over the blue water in the brilliant sunlight, and we played cricket with the passengers"

Victoria Drummond

Marine Engineer
First British Female Marine Engineer

Victoria Drummond was born at Megginch Castle, Perthshire on 18 October 1894, and named after her godmother, Queen Victoria. From a young age, Victoria was fascinated by machines and engineering, and would visit a local engineering works to see steam and petrol engines being built.

When Victoria was 22 years old, she started an apprenticeship at the Northern Garage in Perth. On three evenings a week, she was taught maths and engineering by a teacher from what is now Abertay University. In 1918, Victoria moved to the Caledon Shipbuilding and Engineering Company in Dundee, where she completed her apprenticeship.

Her first assignment on a ship came when she worked for the Blue Funnel line, initially in the engineering office, and then finally on the passenger liner Anchises, as Tenth Engineer. She served on the ship until 1924, travelling to Australia and China. On her return home, she told her family of her experiences,

"There was so much to tell, so much to talk about that I never thought three weeks could pass so fast. I felt quite proud of myself, having made a voyage half round the world as Tenth Engineer. No one ever thought I would stick it out, but I did".

After qualifying as a Second Engineer, she was unable to find work in this position, taking instead a job as Fifth Engineer, which took her to East Africa, India and Ceylon, which she did for some time before going ashore to live and work in London.

While she was ashore, Victoria attempted the Chief Engineer examination, but each attempt failed. She became convinced that the Board of Trades failed her because she was a woman.

At the outbreak of World War II, Victoria returned to sea as a Second Engineer, although she again had difficulty finding a ship to hire her. She was advised to try a foreign a ship, and after some time on an Middle Eastern ship, found work on a ship from Panama, the *Bonita*. On 25 August 1940, *Bonita* was in North Atlantic, around 400 miles (640km) from land, when they were attacked by a German aircraft.

Victoria's actions during the attack, when she was in sole control of the engine room, kept the ship running, and enabled them to escape. She was celebrated as a hero on her arrival in USA, and was later awarded an MBE and the Lloyd's War Medal for Bravery at Sea.

In 1941, Victoria passed the Panama Chief Engineer exam. This was a written exam, where the examiners couldn't tell if the candidate was a man or a woman. However, in the UK, she continued to sit and fail the exam. During the war, the Board of Trade granted Chief

Engineer certificates to experienced Second Engineers, only requiring them to pass an oral exam. They would not allow Victoria to take this exam, and suggested she should take a shore job as an instructor. Victoria's response, that she was more than qualified, and that she had already taken control of the engine room under enemy fire fell on deaf ears.

"It was no good though. I had all the answers. I was a better and more experienced engineer than many then serving under Chief's tickets. But I was a woman and they would not let me pass the exam".

By the end of her career, Victoria had applied for and failed the exam 37 times. The examiners would fail all candidates who sat the exam with her, to avoid being accused of failing her because she was a woman. In fact, when word got around that she intended to take her test on a specific day, men would postpone their exams, rather than sit the test on the same day as Victoria!

In 1961, at the age of 67 years, Victoria sailed aboard her last ship, although she didn't know it at the time. After going ashore, she lived in London with her sisters, and attended the annual meetings of the Institute of Marine Engineers. Victoria died on Christmas Day,

1978 and was buried at Megginch Castle, alongside her sisters and her parents.

In the 40 years of her career, Victoria made 49 ocean-going voyages, winning the respect and support of most of her fellow officers and crew. The first woman Marine Engineer, and the first female member of the Institute of Marine Engineers was later honoured by having a room at the Institute named after her - the Victoria Drummond Room.

BARBARA HILLARY

JUMP! MAG

"Don't forget the bridge that brought you across"

Barbara Hillary

Polar Explorer

First African American Woman to Ski to North Pole

Barbara Hillary started exploring when most people start slowing down. At the age of 75 years, she was the first African American woman to travel to the North Pole.

Barbara was born on 12 June, 1931, and raised in Harlem, New York. Her father died when she was a baby, and her mother brought Barbara and her sister up alone. Her mother was strict, and the family didn't have a lot of money, but the girls never felt that they were missing anything.

Barbara worked as a nurse for 55 years, and travelled in her spare time. As she got older, she began to lose interest in typical holiday destinations. When she was 61 years old, she travelled for the first time alone, on a trip to Guyana, South America.

When she was 67 years old, she survived lung cancer, but this didn't slow her down. After her retirement, she saw an advert to photograph polar bears in Canada, and jumped at the chance.

She went on to learn dog sledding, and how to drive a snowmobile. When she heard that no African American woman had ever been to the North Pole, she decided to be the first!

She sought help and advice from Robert Russel, the founder of a travel company which took people like Barbara on adventures. His company helped customers to travel to the North Pole in various ways, including being dropped off via helicopter. Barbara wasn't taking the easy way out, but if she wanted to ski to the North Pole, she'd have to learn to ski first! "It wasn't a popular sport in Harlem", she joked.

The plan was ambitious, not only because she needed to raise money to pay for the trip, but also because she had to get fit enough for the three day trek, which would involve skiing 8 to 10 hours a day, towing a 25kg sledge. She hired a personal trainer, worked out at the gym, and ate loads of vegetables!

When she finally arrived at the North Pole, her guide said, "Barbara, you are now standing at the top of the world". Forgetting for a moment, the extreme cold, Barbara removed her gloves to give him a thumbs-up, which led to a bit of frostbite, but even that couldn't dull the joy of her amazing achievement.

Not content with being the first African American woman to travel to the North Pole, she resolved to ski to the South Pole, which she reached on 31 January 2011. Since then, Barbara has been travelling around USA, talking to people about her adventures, inspiring others, and sharing her wisdom.

She dedicated the expedition to her mother, saying,

"Never forget the bridge that brought you across".

KIRA SALAK

JUMP! MAG

"Sleep in the Sahara and you can see every star in the graceful curve of Orion's bow, the great sweep of the Milky Way at his back"

Kira Salek

Writer, Journalist, Explorer
First Woman to Kayak 600 miles down Niger River

Kira Salak was born on 4 September 1971 in Chicago, USA. Kira started writing when she was just six years old, and was always keen at sports, particularly running, even aiming to join the national and Olympic teams.

Then she discovered her true love - adventure!

When Kira was 19 years old, she studied in Netherlands, and took the opportunity to discover Europe by rail. Travelling around the continent gave her the confidence to plan a more adventurous trip, to backpack alone around eastern and central Africa and Madagascar.

"Ever since I was a child, when someone tells me I can't do something, it just empowers me all the more. People's doubts in my ability only strengthen my resolve. When they say I can't accomplish a challenge, I just eat that up."

After working in a factory for some time, to earn enough money to finance her trip, she backpacked across Papua New Guinea, the first woman to have done this. During her trip, she faced danger and hardship, but also learned a lot about herself.

After writing a book about her trip, called "Four Corners", she was asked by National Geographic to write about future adventures.

Over the years, she has travelled to some of the most dangerous and remote countries in the world, including

Mozambique, Iran, Rwanda, Peru, Bangladesh and Borneo. Many of the countries Kira explores are unused to solo women travellers, and the response from local inhabitants has ranged from aggression to bemusement, admiration and humour.

"I get a lot of raised eyebrows from the men. But on my trip down the Niger River, the village women crowded on the shore and raised their hands in a cheer. They yelled out, 'Femme forte' [strong woman] and cheered for me as I paddled by."

Despite facing danger and various illnesses such as malaria, dysentery and cholera, Kira is still optimistic about her trips and the people she encounters, saying that even in the most remote areas, she always finds some common ground with the villagers she meets.

"When you get beyond politics and superficial cultural differences, people all want the same things: peace, happiness, success for their children, and the best standard of life".

Kira was the first documented person to kayak solo 600 miles down West Africa's Niger River, and she cycled 100 miles across Alaska to the Arctic Ocean.

Her adventures, and her writing, have inspired people around the world, and led to her being described as a "real-life Lara Croft".

HARRIET CHALMER ADAMS

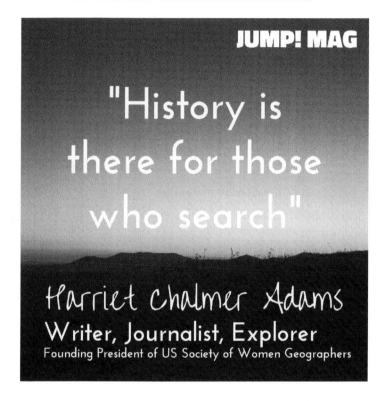

"History is there for those who search"

Harriet Chalmer Adams
Writer, Journalist, Explorer
Founding President of US Society of Women Geographers

JUMP! MAG

Harriet Chalmers was born in California, USA on 22 October 1875. Her love of adventure was fostered at a young age. When she was eight years old, she explored the state of California with her father, riding through the San Joaquin and the Sacramento valleys, and along the

California coast.

"That journey made me over, from a domestic little girl fond of knitting and skipping rope to one who wished to go to the ends of the earth and to see and study the people of all lands"

When she was eleven years old, Harriet swam out to a wooden platform, around 250 yards from the shore at Santa Cruz, then returned to the beach. Harriet was delighted when her swim in the icy waters of the Pacific was reported in the local newspaper.

Harriet loved to read adventure stories and declared, 'Someday I'm going to visit that land. And then I will write my own adventures!"

When she was fourteen years old, she and her father spent a year exploring California from the Oregon border to Mexico, much of the journey along the Sierra Nevada mountain range. Her father taught her many of the skills she would later need in her expeditions, such as how to make observations, and to retain the impressions of the places she visited.

When she married Franklin Pierce Adams in 1899, she found a kindred spirit, a fellow explorer. They were delighted when Frank found a job in Mexico, surveying the country's mines. Harriet loved to explore the countryside, and the ancient Indian and Mayan sites.

She discovered that the stories she'd learned from history books in US were often very different to the ones told in Mexico.

In 1904, Frank accepted a job in Latin America, and the couple began to arrange their trip. Harriet planned to write and lecture about the journey, and learned photography, to better document what they saw. She wrote daily in a travel journal, and sent regular long letters home, which helped her write her later articles.

Over the next two years, they climbed the Andes, canoed through the Amazon and walked through the jungle - traversing El Salvador, Equador, Peru, Bolivia, Chile, Argentina, Paraguay, Brazil, Venezuela and Columbia.

Harriet had a talent for languages, was fluent in Portuguese, Spanish, Italian, German and French, and she easily learned the basics of several native languages.

On their return to the US, Harriet lectured at the National Geographic Society, and began publishing her articles in various newspapers and magazines, which enabled them to continue travelling, first to Cuba, and then on to Asia. Harriet was fascinated by the languages of South America, and wished to trace Asian roots of Native Americas.

During World War I, Harriet worked as a war correspondent in France, and was the only woman to report from the trenches.

Since the US Geographical Society did not allow women members, Harriet and some friends decided to form their own - the Society of Woman Geographers, of which she was chosen as the first president.

In 1926, a fall off a cliff resulted in a terrible injury. Told by doctors that she would never walk again, Harriet spent two years strapped to a board, encased in a plaster cast and steel braces, giving her body time to heal.

The determination, bravery and good humour that she'd shown during her adventures saw her through this horrible experience, and in 1928 she proved the doctors wrong, and learned to walk again.

When Frank retired in 1934, they moved to Spain and

travelled throughout Europe and the Middle East. In 1936, Harriet died in Nice, France, after a short but serious illness. Harriet's lasting legacies, her writing and the society that she helped found, remain a source of inspiration and advice for the adventurers who came after her.

ELLA MAILLART

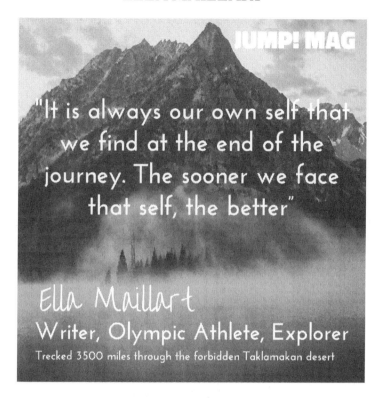

JUMP! MAG

"It is always our own self that we find at the end of the journey. The sooner we face that self, the better"

Ella Maillart

Writer, Olympic Athlete, Explorer
Trecked 3500 miles through the forbidden Taklamakan desert

Born in 1903 in Geneva, Switzerland, Ella Maillart was a phenomenal sportswoman. From an early age, her mother took her skiing in the Swiss Alps, and she learned to sail on Lake Geneva with her childhood friend Hermine (Miette) de Saussure.

Miette and Kini (as Ella was known to her friends) won their first boat race when they were thirteen years old, and at sixteen, Ella became the founder of the first women's field hockey club in Switzerland. The friends skied in winter, sailed in the summer, read books all year around, and dreamed of adventure.

When Miette bought a 21-foot boat, Perlette, the friends finally left Geneva with two other young women, bound for Corsica, Sardinia and Sicily, and then on to the Ionian Islands and Ithaca. Their plan to sail across the Atlantic had to be abandoned when Miette fell ill.

Ella worked for some time on English yachts sailing the Atlantic, and represented Switzerland in the single-handed sailing competition at the Olympic Games of 1924, before trying out various jobs, including a model in Paris, a French teacher in Wales, an actress in a ski film, and a stunt-woman in Berlin! She was a member of the Swiss national skiing team, and competed in World Championship races from 1931 to 1934.

In 1930, Ella travelled to Moscow, and joined a group of students on a trip to the Caucasus, the first of many trips to the region. She wrote about her travels through

Kirghizistan, Kazakstan, Uzbekistan, Turkestan, and the T'ien Shan mountain range (Celestial Mountains). She could see the Taklamakan desert in the distance, an area of China forbidden for travellers, and resolved to return to explore the area. Her book Turkestan Solo detailed her amazing journey.

The newspaper Le Petit Parisien sent Ella to China to explore Manchuria in 1934, where she met Peter Fleming, a journalist from England. They embarked on a 3,500 mile trip west from what was then Peking (now called Beijing) through the Taklamakan desert and Sinkiang, which was at that time forbidden to foreigners, then on to Kashmir. It was a journey that took seven months, and it is said that Ella prepared by taking

"two pounds of marmalade, a rifle, a bottle of Worcestershire sauce, writing paper, a Leica camera".

She continued to travel for many years, through Turkey, India, Iran and Afghanistan, and many other countries along the way. During World War II, she lived in India, where she studied Hindu philosophy, which brought her great peace.

At the end of the war, Ella returned to Chandolin in the Swiss Alps, where she spent her summers. From 1957, she organised cultural tours to various Asian countries, taking small groups of tourists. At the age of 83 years, she went on her last major expedition to Tibet. Ella died in Chandolin, Switzerland on 27 March 1997.

Ella's travel motto was, 'Nobody can go? Then I shall go', and she certainly lived up to that aim, travelling through restricted territories, and writing fascinating accounts of her journeys that will delight readers for many years.

Printed in Great Britain
by Amazon